Military Tech

MILITARY ANIMALS

JULIA GARSTECKI

BLACK RABBIT BOOKS

Bolt is published by Black Rabbit Books
P.O. Box 3263, Mankato, Minnesota, 56002.
www.blackrabbitbooks.com

Marysa Storm, editor; Michael Sellner, designer;
Omay Ayres, photo researcher

Library of Congress Cataloging-in-Publication Data
Names: Garstecki, Julia, author.
Title: Military animals / by Julia Garstecki.
Description: Mankato, Minnesota : Black Rabbit Books, [2018] | Series: Bolt. Military tech | Includes bibliographical references and index. | Audience: Grades 4-6. | Audience: Ages 9-12.
Identifiers: LCCN 2016049966 (print) | LCCN 2016050307 (ebook) | ISBN 9781680721638 (library binding) | ISBN 9781680722277 (e-book)
Subjects: LCSH: Animals–War use–Juvenile literature.
Classification: LCC UH87 .G37 2018 (print) | LCC UH87 (ebook) | DDC 355.4/24-dc23
LC record available at https://lccn.loc.gov/2016049966

Printed in the United States at CG Book Printers,
North Mankato, Minnesota, 56003. 3/17

Image Credits

Alamy: 615 collection, 4–5; Eric Nathan, 12, 13 (bottom); Stocktrek Images, 6; VICTOR HABBICK VISIONS / Science Photo Library, 21 (bottom); Z2A1, 29; AP Images: Oliver Ehmig/Solent News / Rex F, 9 (bottom); Dreamstime: Pzaxe, 3, 25; Getty Images: AFP, 10–11; Barcoft Media, 16–17, 18; CARL DE SOUZA / Stringer, 13 (top); Stacy Pearsall, Cover; http://www.af.mil/: US Airforce, 9 (top); https://www.army.mil/photos: The U.S. Army, 10; http://navy.mil: 1st Class Brien Aho, 1; news.berkeley.edu/2015/03/16/beetle-backpack-steering-muscle: University of California, Berkeley, 22–23; Shutterstock: Fer Gregory, 15; Josh McCann, 26–27; MURGIV, 32; paula french, 14; Rosa Jay, 31; Tony Campbell, 21 (top)

CONTENTS

CHAPTER 1
Animals in Action. 4

CHAPTER 2
Land and Sea Animals. 8

CHAPTER 3
Animals in the Sky. . . .20

CHAPTER 4
Animals in the Future. 24

Other Resources. 30

Animals in ACTION

A U.S. soldier sends Layka, a military dog, to search a building. The dog sniffs for bombs and enemies. Suddenly, an enemy attacks. He shoots Layka four times. But that doesn't stop her. Layka jumps the attacker. She holds him down. He can't shoot nearby soldiers.

Lakya is just one of many animals that have helped soldiers. Militaries around the world use dogs and other animals.

Animals Helping Soldiers

Military animals do many jobs. Some search for bombs. Others guard places. Big or small, animals help soldiers do their jobs.

Layka survived the attack. It took seven hours of surgery to save her. One of her legs had to be removed.

CHAPTER 2

Land and Sea ANIMALS

Dogs are excellent military animals. They are smart and **loyal**. Dogs have a strong sense of smell too. They can be trained to find bombs. Their bark can warn people. Trainers teach many dogs, such as Layka, to attack. The dogs keep soldiers safe. They make soldiers happy in tough situations too.

Some dogs jump from airplanes with soldiers.

U.S. MILITARY DOGS

By the Numbers

ABOUT 50 PERCENT

AMOUNT OF DOGS THAT COMPLETE TRAINING

10 to 12 YEARS

HOW LONG DOGS SERVE

98 PERCENT

HOW OFTEN DOGS' DETECTION SKILLS ARE RIGHT

$20,000 TO $40,000

COST TO TRAIN A DOG

Bomb-Sniffing Rats

Rats can be trained to find bombs too. Like dogs, rats have a good sense of smell. Because they are small, rats can sniff for bombs in tight spaces. They can go where dogs cannot.

The U.S. military has trained rats. People also train and use rats in African and Asian countries. In places such as Cambodia, giant African pouched rats search for **mines**.

GIANT

African Pouched Rat

WEIGHS
2 to 3 pounds
(.9 to 1.4 kilograms)

LIVES UP TO 8 YEARS

TRAINING COSTS ABOUT $6,500

Number of Genes Used for Smelling

elephant
2,000

rat
1,200

dog
1,000

human
400

Excellent Elephants

Dogs and rats both have excellent noses. But elephants' noses are even better. Elephants can smell water from miles away.

The U.S. Army is studying elephants. They are teaching elephants to signal when they smell **TNT**. When an elephant smells TNT, it raises its front leg.

Elephants won't be taken to war zones. Instead, dirt samples could be sent to them.

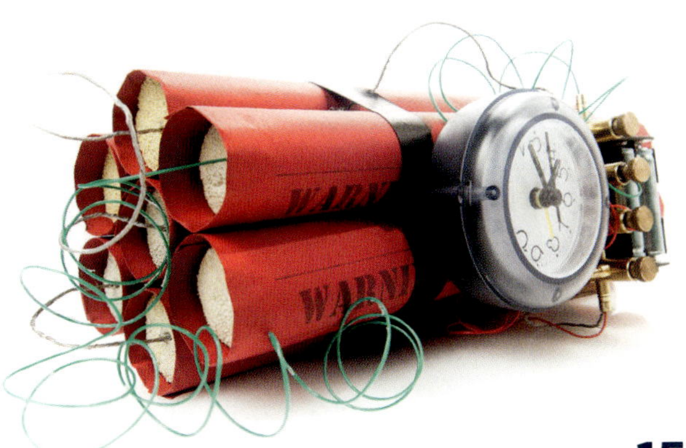

Animals Underwater

Soldiers use underwater animals too. The U.S. and Russian navies train dolphins and sea lions.

Dolphins are fast swimmers. They're smart too. Dolphins are trained to find underwater mines. The animals use **echolocation** to find them. When dolphins find bombs, they swim up to soldiers. The soldiers give the animals markers. The dolphins then tag the bombs' positions.

Top Swim Speeds

Sneaky Sea Lions

Sea lions can see well underwater. They guard water near military bases. They watch for strangers. Some are even trained to catch people. These sea lions swim with clamps. They quickly attach the clamps to divers' legs. Soldiers then pull in the divers.

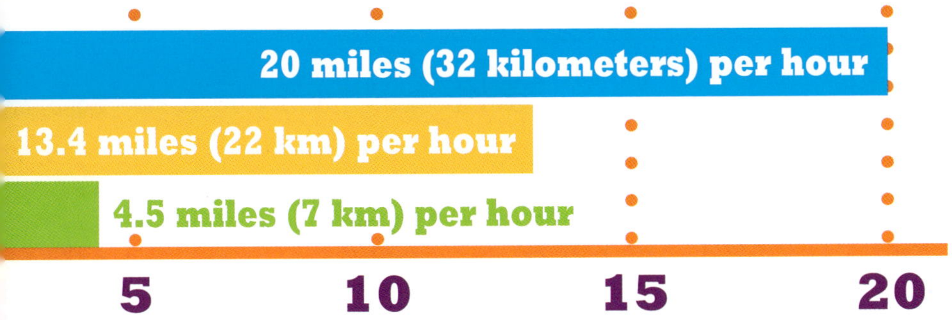

CHAPTER 3

ANIMALS in the Sky

Animals that fly can also have military jobs. Scientists are working with bees. Bees have a good sense of smell. People can train bees to expect food when they smell TNT. This training teaches bees to go where they smell TNT.

Bees could be taken to war zones. Soldiers would watch where they swarm. If they swarm over a spot, a bomb could be there.

People can attach tiny computer chips to beetles. Computers then send messages to the chips. The messages tell the bugs where to fly. Someday, these bugs could carry small cameras. They would be used as spies.

CYBORG BEETLES

Beetles make good cyborg bugs. They are stronger than flies or moths. They can carry more weight.

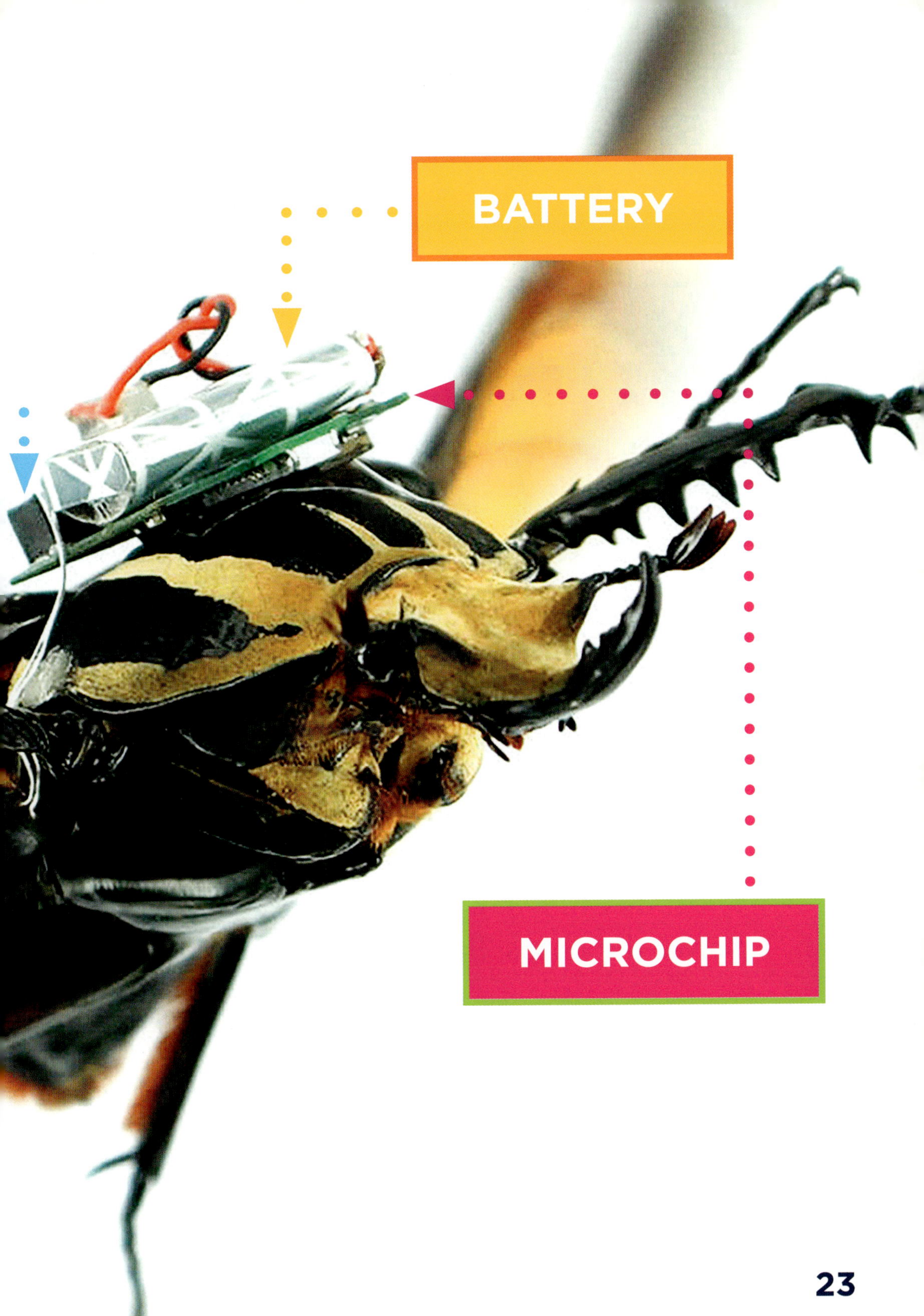
BATTERY
MICROCHIP

CHAPTER 4

Animals in the FUTURE

Scientists are working on new and better ways to use animals. Computer chips attached to bugs aren't always **reliable**. People are researching putting chips inside young bugs. As the bugs grow, the chips will become part of them. Their bodies will power the chips. People could then control the bugs.

Replaced by Robots

Robot animals will be used in the future too. Future **drones** will be fast and small, just like bugs. They may look like them too.

Other machines will copy what animals do. Some machines might smell as well as elephants. Others could carry gear across rocky hills. They would move like mules.

Amazing Animals

Militaries all over the world use animals. Like soldiers, animals have many jobs. Some work in the field. Others **inspire** technology. They help keep people safe.

GLOSSARY

cyborg (SAHY-bawrg)—a person or animal whose body contains mechanical or electrical devices

detection (dih-TEK-shuhn)—discovery of something

drone (DRON)—an unmanned aircraft or ship guided by remote control or onboard computer

echolocation (eh-ko-lo-KAY-shun)—a process of bouncing sound waves off something to determine where it is

gene (JEEN)—a part of a cell that controls or influences a bodily trait or activity

inspire (in-SPIHR)—to give someone an idea about what to do or make

loyal (LOY-uhl)—having complete support for someone or something

mine (MAHYN)—a bomb that is placed in the ground or in water and that explodes when it is touched

reliable (ri-LAHY-uh-buhl)—able to be trusted to do or provide what is needed

TNT—a very powerful explosive

LEARN MORE

BOOKS

Furstinger, Nancy. *Paws of Courage: True Tales of Heroic Dogs that Protect and Serve.* Washington, D.C.: National Geographic, 2016.

Goldish, Meish. *Skydiving Dogs.* Dog Heroes. New York: Bearport Publishing, 2014.

Mooney, Carla. *Remarkable Military Animals.* Ready for Military Action. Minneapolis: Core Library, an imprint of Abdo Publishing, 2015.

WEBSITES

10 Things You May Not Know About Military Dogs
barkpost.com/10-things-about-military-dogs/

Animal Veterans
kids.nationalgeographic.com/explore/history/veterans-day/

U.S. Navy Marine Mammal Program
www.public.navy.mil/Spawar/Pacific/71500/Pages/Animals.aspx

INDEX

B

bees, 20

beetles, 21, 22–23

C

costs, 11, 13

D

dogs, 4, 7, 8, 9, 10–11, 12, 14, 15

dolphins, 16, 18–19

E

elephants, 14, 15, 27

R

rats, 12–13, 14, 15

robots, 27

S

sea lions, 16, 18–19